RET
YOUR HEART
THOUGHTS FROM ST AUGUSTINE

COMPILED BY
Ben O'Rourke OSA

Prayers and reflections
from the writings of
Augustine of Hippo

Published by
Augustinian Press UK
Clare Priory
Suffolk CO10 8NX

©1995 Augustinian Press UK
First published 1995
New Edition 2002
First reprint 2003
Second reprint 2007

ISBN 0 9542807 0 9

'God speaks to us in the great silence of the heart.'

The most important journey in life is the journey inwards, to the depths of our own being.

Augustine constantly calls us to return to our hearts. Only there, he says, will we find rest and peace for our unquiet souls. And if we journey to the centre of our being we shall find our true selves, and we shall find God. For He has made his home in us.

I hope that these thoughts from Augustine will help us on that journey inward, to the stillness within, where we shall find rest and peace in God.

Ben O'Rourke OSA
Clare Priory, Suffolk
May 2002

'In the silence we find God.'

Enter then into your heart
and if you have faith
you will find Christ there.
There He speaks
to you.
I the preacher
must raise my voice,
but He instructs you
more effectively
in the silence.
I speak in sounding words.
He speaks
within.

It is difficult in a crowd
to see Christ.
Our soul needs solitude.
In solitude,
if we are attentive,
God allows himself to be seen.
In the crowd
we find noise.
In the silence
we find God.

If only our minds
could be held steady,
they would be still
for a while,
and for that short moment
we would glimpse
the splendour
of eternity
which is forever still.

When we pray
we have no need
of spoken word.
Sometimes the tongue is silent
and the soul is sighing.
That means that God
is being prayed to inside,
in the room of your heart.

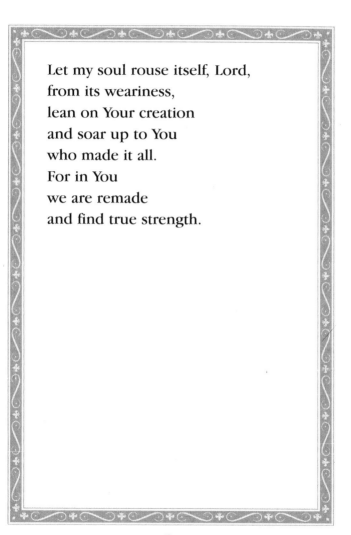

Let my soul rouse itself, Lord,
from its weariness,
lean on Your creation
and soar up to You
who made it all.
For in You
we are remade
and find true strength.

God speaks to us
in the great silence
of the heart.

The Word of God
is never silent though
He is not always heard.

Enter into yourself.
Leave behind all noise
and confusion.
Look within yourself
and see whether there be
some sweet hidden place within
where you can be free
from noise and argument,
where you need not be carrying on
your disputes, and planning
to have your own stubborn way.
Hear the word in quietness
that you may understand it.

Imagine that God
wants to fill you up
with honey.
But if you are already
full of vinegar,
where will you put the honey?
The heart must be emptied
and washed out,
made clean and scoured,
hard work though it may be,
so that it be made ready
for something else,
whatever it may be.

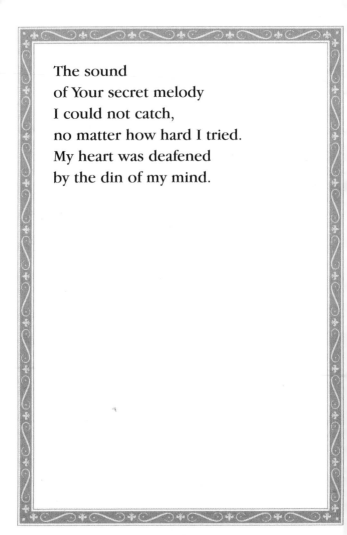

The sound
of Your secret melody
I could not catch,
no matter how hard I tried.
My heart was deafened
by the din of my mind.

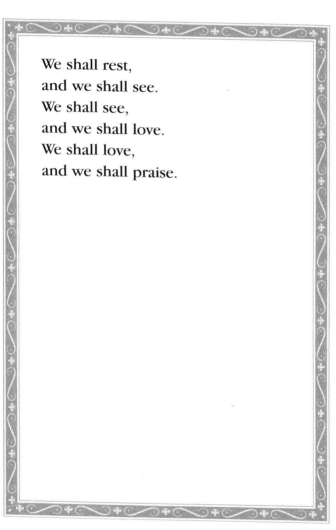

We shall rest,
and we shall see.
We shall see,
and we shall love.
We shall love,
and we shall praise.

God is delight
and we rest in delight with Him,
called home from the noise
that is around us
to the joys that are silent.
Why do we rush about
to the top of heaven
and the bottom of earth
looking for Him
who is here at home with us,
if only we could be
with Him?

'Let Christ speak to you within.'

He bade me shut the door
of our secret chamber
and pray in secret,
that is in the soundless
secret places of our hearts.
For we pray to Him
in the silence
of our hearts.

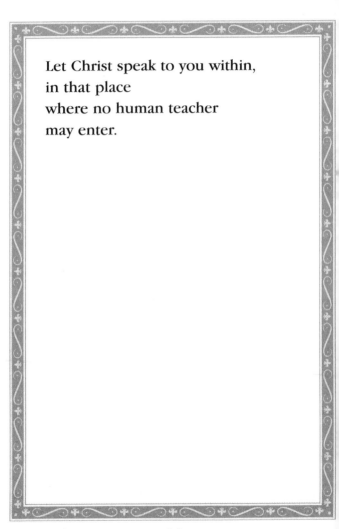

Let Christ speak to you within,
in that place
where no human teacher
may enter.

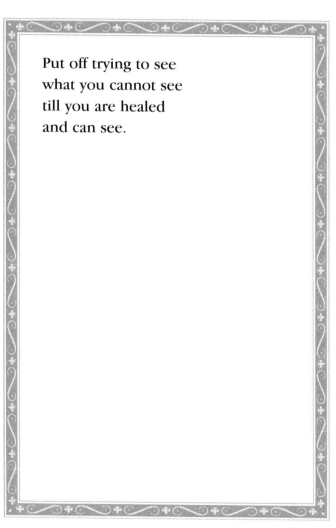

Put off trying to see
what you cannot see
till you are healed
and can see.

When we confess to You,
we are not revealing to You
what lies in our hearts.
For Your gaze penetrates
even a heart that is
locked against You.
Nor can a heart that is hardened
resist Your touch.
You unbind the heart
when You choose,
by Your compassion
or by Your angel.
No one can hide
from the warmth of Your love.

You listen to all who pray to You.
And You answer them all.
You answer clearly,
but not all hear You clearly.
All ask what they want,
but do not always hear
the answer they want.
Your best servants are those
who are not so much concerned
to hear from You
what they will,
as to will
what they hear
from You.

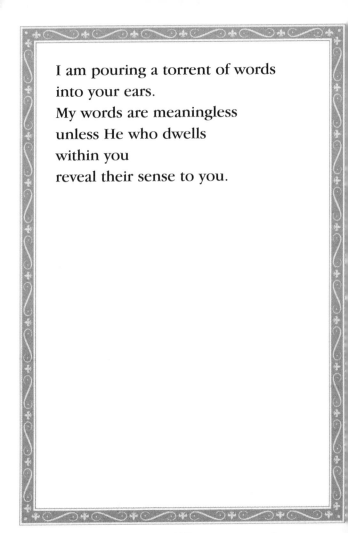

I am pouring a torrent of words
into your ears.
My words are meaningless
unless He who dwells
within you
reveal their sense to you.

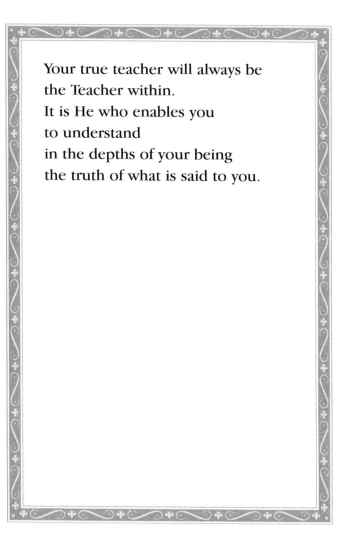

Your true teacher will always be
the Teacher within.
It is He who enables you
to understand
in the depths of your being
the truth of what is said to you.

Wheresoever you are,
wheresoever you may be praying,
He who hears you is within you,
hidden within.
For He who hears you
is not merely by your side,
and you have no need
to go wandering about,
no need
to be reaching out to God
as though you would touch Him
with your hands.
Wheresoever you are,
wheresoever you may be praying,
He who hears you is within you,
hidden within.

Wait for the Lord.
Be firm.
Let your heart take courage
and wait for the Lord.
What does it mean,
wait for the Lord?
It means
that you may receive His gifts
when He gives them,
instead of demanding them
when you want them.
The time for giving
has not yet come.
He has waited for you,
and so you must wait
for Him.

Do not wish
to ask anything of God
except God.
Love Him
without seeking gain.
Desire Him alone.
This is to love God
without seeking gain:
to hope for God from God,
to wish to be filled with God,
to be satiated by Him.

'In your inner self Christ has made his home.'

Come back with me to the heart.
Get your heart ready to see God.
The one to whom God speaks
is within.
It is the inner person
in whom Christ resides.

He bids you return to Him,
to that place within,
where peace abides,
peace that is never disturbed;
to that place from which
Love never departs,
unless you depart from it.
Make your home in that place.
Surrender to Him
what you have,
since all came from Him.

You alone are always present,
even to those who have set
themselves apart from You.
Let them turn back
and look for You.
They will find that You
have not deserted them
as they have deserted You.
Let them turn back
and they will find You
in their hearts.

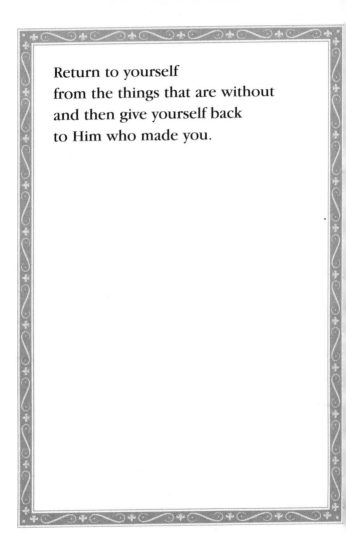

Return to yourself
from the things that are without
and then give yourself back
to Him who made you.

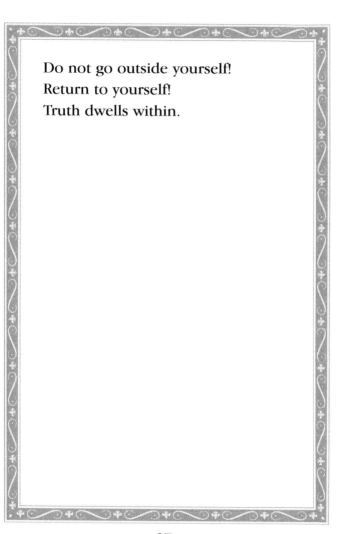

Do not go outside yourself!
Return to yourself!
Truth dwells within.

Those who try to find joy
in things outside themselves
find only frustration and emptiness.
They waste themselves
on the passing pleasures
of the moment.
Their hearts are starved.
But it was in my inmost heart,
it was there that You, Lord,
had made me begin to love You
and had made me glad at heart.

For the light was within
while I looked
on the world outside.
I found no place outside
where I might rest,
no haven where I might feel
myself satisfied and content.
Nor would the things around me
let me turn back
where I might find
contentment and satisfaction.

The Christian may sometimes envy
those who have renounced
the cares of the world for
the supposed calm of the desert;
but those who live in the world
may at any time
find the true desert within,
where no one enters,
where there is no one else
but God.

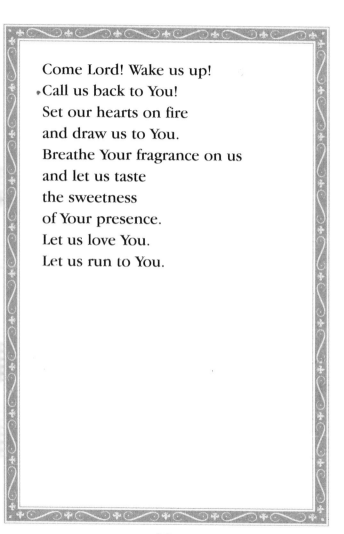

Come Lord! Wake us up!
Call us back to You!
Set our hearts on fire
and draw us to You.
Breathe Your fragrance on us
and let us taste
the sweetness
of Your presence.
Let us love You.
Let us run to You.

Why do you want to drift
so far away from yourself?
By wandering away
you lose yourself.
Turn back from
your idle wandering.
Return to your Lord.
He is waiting.
You have become a stranger
to yourself.
You do not recognise yourself.
And you seek for Him
who created you!
Come back to your heart.
In your inner self
Christ has made his home.
In your inner self you will be
renewed in God's image.
And in his image
you will recognise your creator.

*'I shall lead you and carry you
on to the end.'*

Soul, surrender to Him now
all your futile searching.
What is withered in you
will flower again.
Your sickness will be healed.
What is fading will be fresh again,
and what is warped made whole
and strong and sound.
And all that is weak in you
will not drag you to the grave.
But your wholeness will abide,
will remain with you before God,
who remains strong
and abides for ever.

At the well where
Our Lord sat down to rest
great mysteries
took place.

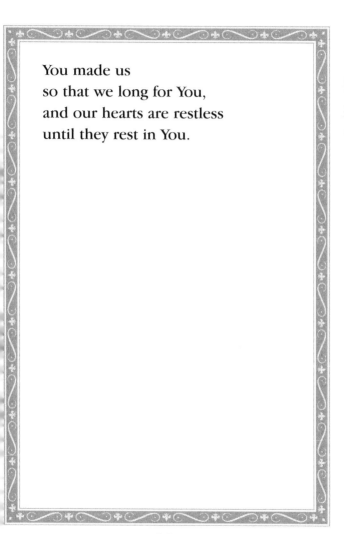

You made us
so that we long for You,
and our hearts are restless
until they rest in You.

I beg you, O Lord my God,
to look upon me and listen to me.
Have pity on me and heal me,
for You see that I have become
a problem to myself,
and this is the sickness
from which I suffer.

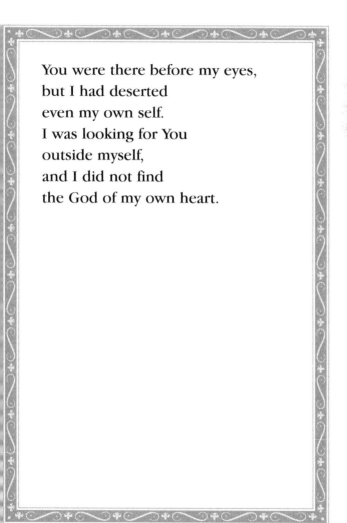

You were there before my eyes,
but I had deserted
even my own self.
I was looking for You
outside myself,
and I did not find
the God of my own heart.

Late have I loved You,
Beauty ever old yet ever new!
Late have I loved You!
You were within me,
but I was outside.
There I sought You,
as I rushed about
among the beautiful things
You had made.
You were with me,
but I was not with You.
The beautiful things of this world

kept me far from You.
You called. You cried.
You burst through my deafness.
You scattered my blindness.
I breathed Your fragrance
and now I pine for You.
I tasted You,
and I hunger and thirst for You.
You touched me,
and I burn with desire
for Your peace.

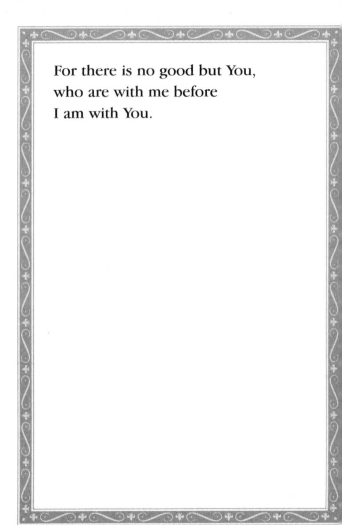

For there is no good but You,
who are with me before
I am with You.

You are the most hidden from us,
and yet the most present
among us.

What crooked paths I trod!
Whichever way my soul turned,
it lay on a bed that was hard,
for in You alone
the soul can rest.
You are there to free us
from our misery,
to set us on Your own path
and to comfort us by saying,
'Run on, for I shall hold you up.
I shall lead you and carry you on
to the end.'

Unknown to me
You caressed my head.
You closed my eyes
lest they see the things
that keep me from You.
I lost for a while
the heavy burden of self
and my madness
was lulled to sleep.
And when I awoke in You
I saw You with utterly
different eyes.

All the time I wanted
to stand and listen.
To listen to Your voice.
But I could not,
because another voice,
the voice of my own ego,
dragged me away.

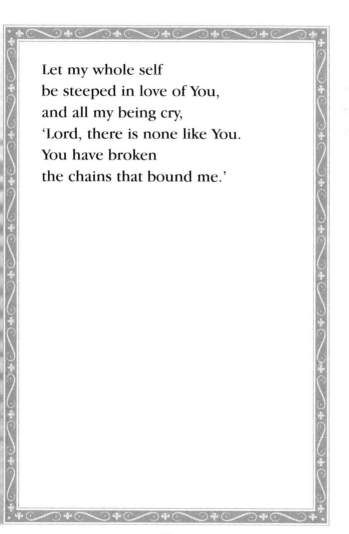

Let my whole self
be steeped in love of You,
and all my being cry,
'Lord, there is none like You.
You have broken
the chains that bound me.'

You saw me
and transformed my ugliness
into beauty.
Like a balm which soothes my pain,
Your hidden touch
healed my self love.
And day by day
You continued to heal me
until the confusion and darkness
were cleared
from the eye of my soul.

*'Let the shelter of Your wings
give us hope.'*

He is in the depths of our heart,
but our heart has forsaken Him.
Stay with Him,
and you shall be safe.
Rest in Him
and you will be at peace.

Tell me Lord, in Your mercy,
what You are to me.
Say to my soul,
'I am the one who saves you.'
Say it that I may hear it.
My heart waits to hear.
Open my heart and say to it
'I am the one who saves you.'
I will run to hear,
run to clasp You to myself.
Do not hide Your face
from me.

O Lord our God,
let the shelter of Your wings
give us hope.
Protect us and uphold us.
When You are our strength
we are strong,
but when our strength
is our own
we are weak.
Let us come home to You,
O God,
for fear that we be lost.

Unless the Lord
helps us carry our burdens,
we shall sink beneath them,
and unless He carries us,
we shall fall to our death.

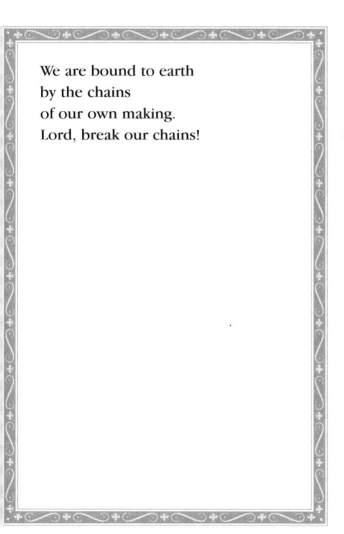

We are bound to earth
by the chains
of our own making.
Lord, break our chains!

God is nearer to us
than we are
to ourselves.

You care for each of us,
as if we were the only one
You had to care for.

Whisper words of truth in my heart,
for You alone speak truth.
I will leave outside
those who do not believe,
letting them stir up the dust
in their own eyes,
while I withdraw to my secret cell
and sing to You hymns of love.
I shall not turn aside
until You gather all that I am
into that holy place of peace,
rescuing me from the world
where I am broken and deformed
and giving me new form
and new strength.

For Christians who fear they are
drowning in the world's business
the worst thing they can do
is panic.
There can be no question of escape
from the situation.
We are many miles from land
and there is no help near.
The one thing we can do
is to withdraw, as it were,
into ourselves,
to find the Christ within,
who is as powerful
to still the inner tempest
as He was to subduc the waves
on the Lake of Galilee.

I find no safe place for myself
save in You,
in whom all my scattered pieces
are gathered together.

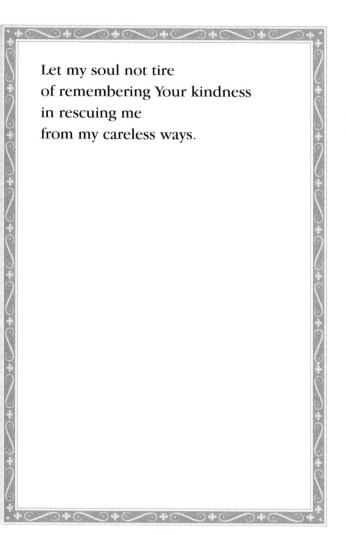

Let my soul not tire
of remembering Your kindness
in rescuing me
from my careless ways.

May I love You!
Love You strongly, deeply.
May I, with all my inner strength,
hold on to You!
That You may keep me
from all danger
now and forever.

He departed from our sight
when He left the world,
so that we should turn
to our hearts
and find Him there.
He departed,
but He is here with us.

Leave it to your maker to ensure,
in ways you don't understand,
that all will be well with you.